Sexidents

learning & healing from sexual mishaps

Copyright © 2024 by Bria Price

All rights reserved.

No portion of this book may be reproduced in any form without written permission from the publisher or author, except as permitted by U.S. copyright law.

I relied on interviews and conversations I had with many people who appear in these pages, as well as my own memory. In some cases I have edited conversations for brevity. To protect the anonymity of certain individuals, I have modified their names.

Please note the information contained within this document is for educational and entertainment purposes only. The content within this book has been derived from various sources. Please consult a licensed professional before attempting any techniques outlined in this book. The author and publisher specifically disclaim all responsibility for any liability, loss or risk, personal or otherwise, that is incurred as a consequence, directly or indirectly, of the use and application of any of the contents of this book.

REAL PEOPLE. REAL STORIES. REAL HEALING.

This book is dedicated to those who believe in the beauty of sex, who may have had that view slightly tarnished accidentally, without realizing the overflow of support available to you to overcome those experiences that make you giggle, embarrass, traumatize, or haunt you to your core.

You aren't alone.

We share similar stories and we'll heal from them together.

Contents

Introduction	*6*
So What Are We About to Do?	*11*
A Party Ain't A Party With You	*14*
Who Goes There!	*21*
Where Do I Stick It?	*25*
A Delicate Flower	*28*
Up In Arms	*32*
Older, And None The Wiser	*38*
Blown	*43*
I Know You're Single Bitch But…	*46*
Who Pulls The Strings?	*51*
Take It At Face Value	*54*
Lend Me Some Sugar	*57*
Resources	*61*
Acknowledgments	*76*

Introduction:

All it took was one steamy and passionate night to ignite the idea of this book.

One dark, summery, and kid-free night, my lover and I decided we were going to let loose sexually. We were going to go hard in the bedroom all night, to make up for lost orgasmic time. See, when you have kids, as plenty of us do, we all know that squeezing in time for hot sex becomes quite a challenge, but this night we were up for it. Tonight was the night where we could just take our time, in the peace and quiet, focus, and deeply feel every stroke, lick, and orgasm that we could offer each other.

Preparation was key for me, so I scheduled my Brazilian bikini wax early that week to get ready for our exciting weekend. Being a woman, I know and understand that beauty is utter and sincere pain…but I took every wax rip with a smile because I just knew it would be worth it that Saturday night. I exfoliated, primmed, and kegeled my way through the week, and before I knew it Saturday night was here.

Ladies, you know how you know you're about to get dicked down and those butterflies begin fluttering so hard that you think you might cum right then and there? Well, they were here, flapping their horny wings, so much so that I wanted to skip dinner and get right to dessert. To be honest, looking back on it, I don't even remember eating.

I probably thought "I can eat later, I need to savor all the alone time I have with my man."

Introduction

So, dinner was done, the house was empty, and the bed was ready to be torn to shreds. We kiss, laugh, and rub our way to the bedroom, salivating at the night to come. It was a nice August night, a cool breeze was flowing throughout our home, and I was so ready for him to get in bed with me.

    We immediately undressed. He cracked open a fresh jar of coconut oil and began rubbing my thighs with it, working his way up to my middle. He spreads my legs, revealing my fresh wax, and makes love to me with his fingers, mixing my juices in with the oil. As he's doing that, he kisses his way up to my nipples, giving them a little love with the coconut oil too. He goes back down to devour me with his mouth for what seemed like a few seconds because I came so quickly. It was that good. One orgasm in and my head was already spinning but we were just getting started. I turned around, doggy style, and he began with slow strokes that quickly heated up.

    All sounds amazing, right? It was. But...here's where it got sticky. Of course, the likelihood of coconut oil getting messy is a matter of fact, especially when it's everywhere. But not a friend, sister, mother, or stranger on the street could've mentally prepared me for what was next. I was in an orgasmic trance.He was hitting the spot I needed from behind so effortlessly, I didn't think I could feel any better than I did in that moment. It was going so good...so good that my body started collapsing into the mattress until I was face down in the sheets, with muffled moans, and blissful tears streaming from my eyes. We were in the groove. In sync. He placed his strong hands on my hips and started bouncing my pelvis from the bed onto his throbbing shaft, in a rhythmic fashion. It was then and there that I realized how dangerous coconut oil could be.

There was so much oil, juices, and love flowing down there that it turned into a slip-and-slide. And before I knew it…his dick slipped into "the wrong hole" and all of my glorious pleasure immediately turned into sheer pain.

  At this point, I know what you're thinking…"Oh, it couldn't have been that bad, people do anal all the time!" That statement is correct. But more than likely, you plan for anal. You get mentally prepared. You want it. Welcome it. Crave it even. And sure, I've tried it out lightyears before, but it was nothing to this capacity. I literally got pounded into! This wasn't a "whoops, wrong hole" moment. This was with the same vigor and strength that he used to fuck my vagina. And yes, I mean *fuck.*
  Due to everything being so slippery, he had no idea where he had entered at that point. And because my face was plastered in the bed already, he couldn't hear my pleas for him to stop. It was after about five or six gut-wrenching, full-dick pumps that my body and his mind registered what was happening and he could *feel* my body tense up in agony. He stopped immediately once he knew but by then it was far too late. All I could do was lay there in the fetal position, literally holding my bare anus, mortified by what just transpired. I could see the complete shock and sorrow written all over his face but his words were muffled behind my "ow, ow, ow, oh my God's." Our special night ended there, but I would soon find that I would carry this night with me for far more days to come.
  The next day, the soreness was a million times worse than the actual pain afflicted the night before. I could barely sit down without wincing in pain. I didn't know what to do about going to the bathroom, so I suffered in even more silence. I felt like I was losing my mind.

Introduction

I didn't know who to talk to or how to overcome this. The recovery time was about 7-10 days for my ass to feel normal again, but mentally it took months to get my sexual confidence back. I was secretly scared of coconut oil for a while and whenever we slipped into that position again, I could feel my body get stiff, as if it were preparing for that particular pain. I stifled the discomfort I felt and did my best to see through it to essentially rewire my body and mind. I've always been a sexual person by nature so I figured if I just got back into the swing of things I could replace the traumatic memory with a more satisfying one. Whenever I felt uncomfortable or scared, I just calmly let my partner know to slow down or change positions. But it was hard to put myself back into a sexual space mentally. I had a few talks with my partner about it, but he didn't technically experience any pain, so he couldn't understand what I felt.

It wasn't until about two weeks later that I cracked. I broke down with my sister after a night of drinking. We've always been close, and our conversations about sex matured as we have. As I was telling her the story, she stopped me mid-climax with a scream."OMG! The same thing just happened to me like a week ago!" I immediately felt relieved. Not because I was happy she was hurt too, but because someone understood the mental and physical transformation I had gone through. We shared our experiences which surprisingly ended in laughter.

By the end of it, we both realized that it was indeed an accident, but talking honestly about it helped us feel more seen, heard, and strong enough to overcome it. If I hadn't talked to her, I'm not sure I would've been able to process it as quickly as I did, let alone at all.

Which is why I wrote this book. For those of us who need to physically, mentally, and emotionally process sexual mishaps by connecting with real experiences from others who also don't wish to do it alone.

Here-
We can heal together.

Chapter One:
So What Are WE About To Do?

This was...I'll say 2012. I'm newly single, just out here mingling and whatnot. My cousin went to East Carolina University where I would always visit him. He had this one friend Brandon, who he brought over to my grandparents' house for Christmas. We started locking eyes and he and I just clicked. Although he did lie to me about his age...that's another story for another time.

We ended up messing around and even exchanged numbers, but eventually, I had to go back home to my starting five. Honey, I kept a starting five okay! If you're dating, you know you have to keep your options open. As excited as I was to be back in my hometown, my eagerness was cut short due to the unfortunate passing of my great-grandmother.

So here I was, after a short year, making my way back down to North Carolina where I would spend another week with my cousin at his school. Just relaxing, partying, and doing what teenagers do. Brandon and I did text back and forth while I was back home, so the sexual tension bubbled up to the brim. When I got back, it exploded. We ended up having sex...and I ended up getting pregnant.

I didn't know that I was pregnant. It didn't hit me until I started feeling sick and I was like "I need to go to Patient First." I just knew I caught something. I'm like what is wrong with me? I wasn't thinking about pregnancy at all.

I was thinking I had the flu because I felt so sick. I felt stuffy and I got constant headaches, so I just knew I had strep throat, a common cold, or the flu. I was expecting to walk out of Patient First with some antibiotics to kill these germs! But instead, I walked out with a positive pregnancy test. So I started doing some math on my calendar like "Wait a minute, let me think back to who was doing what during this time and where I was." Come to find out, it was Brandon's baby. However, one of the guys in my starting five back home was rummaging through my stuff and found the paper from Patient First stating that I was pregnant. Like, who does that? Men are crazier than women! So, I had to think quickly on my feet and I was just like "Oh yeah I'm pregnant, so what are we about to do?"

I already knew he didn't want a baby because I was 19 at the time and I didn't want a kid either. So again, I'm like "What are *we* about to do?" and he's like "I'm going to help you pay for this abortion." All I could respond with was "Okay."

I ended up never telling Brandon that I had gotten pregnant by him, although we did text here and there after I got the abortion. I just figured I would take that shit to the grave, which is ironic because sadly he ended up dying a few years later.

As expected, the other guy I was dealing with who ended up paying for the abortion started to question things. He began asking things like "How did it happen? And when?" and I'm just like "I don't know. They say "x" amount of weeks and you're the only one I've been dealing with." Until this day, he's never figured out that it wasn't his baby. He would follow me on various social media sites and I just always ended up blocking him.

*So What Are **WE** About To Do?*

I've never come clean about it. The only people that know are my best friend and another guy I was dating in my starting five. I guess you could say I got pregnant by somebody else and made someone else pay for it. This to me is considered an sexident because I wasn't supposed to be having sex with Brandon in the first place since he was my cousin's best friend. So the real tea is...I shouldn't have been fucking him! Karma came back so quickly for me. This happened in 2012 but I didn't tell anyone or speak about it until about maybe 2015-2016. It did cross my mind when I would see Brandon around the holidays but I really thought about it when he died. It was like damn, this isn't something I would ever be able to share with him once I felt comfortable enough to open up like I am now.

It kind of felt like, not a dark cloud following me, but something similar to that. It just felt like the weight was on my shoulders. I felt kind of guilty. It's like damn, I did lie to this one boy, making him think he was the only one when he wasn't. I also lied to him and told him that by me being pregnant, it was his baby, when I knew good and got damn well that it wasn't. But I only allowed him to pay for it because one, he snooped through my stuff, and two, I knew Brandon didn't have any money and abortions are expensive! I just didn't want to pay for that by myself. Not only that, but I was young and still on my mom's insurance and that was something I just didn't want her in my business about. So I just knew I had to find an alternate way. I guess his snooping through my stuff was a blessing and a curse.

The moral of the story is...we all have skeletons. **Some are accidental, some with purpose.**

Chapter Two:
A Party Ain't A Party With You

I was with this guy Bryan for a while and I thought that I, you know...fell in love with this person. I thought that he completed me and I was foolishly mistaken. Looking back, our relationship was based on what I could do for him and not what he could do for me. It was very one-sided and confusing. It was as if communication wasn't being communicated intentionally. In a nutshell, I feel like I was manipulated in the situation but this was nothing but a learning experience.

One day Bryan decided he randomly wanted to have "this party," or get together if you will, for his friends. He asked me if I could help him put it together and host it. At the time obviously, I was like "Oh this is a big step in our relationship." We're putting a party together for people and letting it be known that we're together, but that wasn't the case.

So I show up to prepare and help him set up. It was fun as we were setting up and I was excited about the party. But then hours pass and the party is here and now there's a whole bunch of different people, specifically gay men there. I feel like red flags were popping up constantly.

There were so many moments I should've listened to myself but I didn't. Like some of the people that were there he had prior relations with, they knew nothing about me, nor had he expressed or shared anything about me. He painted a picture as if I was just his friend helping or collaborating with him for this party.

A Party Ain't A Party With You

All night I was noticing different things. He would casually leave and then other people would leave and I would randomly notice that they would pop back up at the same time. You know, me being the person I am, I just kind of ignored it and kept going.

But after a while, you can't ignore so many things. At one point I just got annoyed with the whole party and situation. I went into his room, closed the door, and went to sleep. I was completely over everything and everyone and I had to go...or I was going to slap the shit out of somebody. I was awakened by him asking me if I was okay. I said, "Of course, I'm fine." That's something I do a lot. I lie about how I'm truly feeling to protect other people's feelings and to avoid arguments in relationship aspects. But I feel like honestly, regardless of if I would have said if I was okay or not, he would've still moved on to the next topic. That was just the vibe that I got. He didn't care if I was mad. He just felt like that was what he was *supposed* to ask.

So incidentally he pops up and he's like "I want you to have some fun with me." Once again, me being who I am and wanting this relationship to work, I'm like "Yeah let's have some fun!" I was excited and glad he was trying to invite me to join some fun. So he hands me some coke to sniff and a pill. You know what? Me being a dumb ass I don't even know what kind of pill it was. I just trusted this person so much that I thought he wouldn't give me anything that would hurt me. Also, we've had past conversations where he's like "Don't ever do any hard drugs without me. I want you to be safe." So I felt like he was well-versed in this kind of lifestyle. I want to say he had already taken the drugs he offered me while I was asleep. He handed me the drugs and right after I took them, he then repeated what he said, "I want you to have some fun with me...and I want you to suck some dick with me." I don't remember fully agreeing to it, I just know I didn't say anything. I was feeling a little high and I was also trying to please him and not disappoint him.

Mind you, at this time it was about 2 or 3 in the morning. Some people had left but the people that were there...were there. So right after he said that one of his friends came into the room and he told me to do things with the friend. He said, "I want to see you suck his dick." His eyes got big and he started smiling like he was excited about this. Now again, I am in a state of mind where I want to please my partner and I want him to be happy, but at the same time being high, so I'm not necessarily thinking logically. While at the same time thinking "Well, if I say no to this...what's going to happen? Is it going to be awkward? Is something weird going to happen to me?" Because again, it wasn't just us in this house, it was multiple people. Apparently, they all knew what this was but me. I think he planned the whole scenario.

So as it was happening, other people started coming into the room and started doing sexual things...then they started doing sexual things to me. He also started doing things with other people and it just became a whole sexual orgy that I didn't intend on getting into. But I was in it... and again on drugs and just not being confident in my own decisions at the time. I just kept going to save face, to be peaceful, and to please my partner. In the sense of the stimulation part, yes things felt good, but in the back of my mind the whole time it did feel weird. It was like, is our relationship becoming stronger or did we just put a pin in the coffin of our relationship by him sharing me with his "friends?"

That was going through my mind the whole time.

Once the "first round" was essentially over, I left the room to go to the bathroom and when I left, I looked to my right (the bathroom was on my left,) and he was making out with this guy very passionately in the middle of the floor. It was weird. You would think I would've realized what I was into once the sex happened but it was at that moment I realized...this is an orgy. Even still, in that moment I just went with the flow because I've always been that type of person.

So I'm in the middle of an orgy with all these different people. Everyone didn't fuck me, but maybe two different people did, and I watched him get fucked...which was interesting. And it also explained why he had fleets in his bathroom that didn't belong to me. A fleet is a device, similar to a douche, that you use to cleanse your anus before sex. He's always randomly had these under his sink and things like that, so at that moment I'm like "Oh okay, so you've been getting fucked." So many different ideas started coming into my head.

For instance, I would clean his apartment sometimes and I would find an open condom wrapper and intentionally leave it in the middle of the floor, so he knows that I saw it. So a lot of things were racing through my head and started to make sense.

So I'm in an orgy and I think it kind of made sex traumatic for me because at that moment I realized sex was not about soul ties anymore or emotional connection, it was just about the act itself. At the time it felt like I was a part of some demonic cult or ring, and it made me feel so weird.

When it was over...it was over. We continued to be friends after that, but fast forward, I realized that he wasn't the person for me. He didn't care about me at all. He only cared about himself and what I could provide for him. It had nothing to do with me. Turns out this situation was the nail in the coffin for our relationship, at least for me.

I ended things with us by not responding to things and slowly backing off. I was at an event months later, and a few of the people who were at that party were there and we started talking. It was brought up to me that they left with Bryan multiple times that night to do sexual things when I wasn't looking. They also let me know they didn't realize we were in a relationship or anything relatively close to one. That to me was confirmation that what we had wasn't anything because nothing about him is trustworthy or promising at all. He just said what he needed to say to keep me around. Seeing those people didn't necessarily bring up any emotional trauma, because I had already moved on and I was with someone new. Plus I had already established that the person who I was with was trash. Their bringing this to me just confirmed my decision and made me realize I have to trust my intuition the first time.

Since then, sex has just been a weird topic for me. Even when it comes to my new relationship, I have very big trust issues and I question everything. When things look weird, I just automatically assume it is. It has made me more cautious and in my mind a lot more. I feel like I'm less naive now because of it. Although it was traumatic, it taught me to trust myself.

Moving on, internalizing what happened, and meditating has helped me get over this situation. Naturally, I'm a person who's more so sad over situations where I feel like I could've done something different. In addition to that, what also helped me heal from this is realizing and understanding that *this* person has issues, *this* person is a narcissist, and *this* person is struggling with whatever trauma he's dealing with and it has affected me in some way. But that's not my cross to bear or my problem. It just made me realize that I need to focus on myself. It wasn't until I started focusing on myself that I found someone new and understood what it meant to truly care about someone.

I'm very cautious about boundaries now. What do I want? Or what does my partner want? I feel like that plays a big role in people's decisions, as far as having sex with other people or feeling like their needs aren't being met. But it all boils down to communication. I'm a very open and creative person, so just tell me what you need and we can probably do it. It also showed me that one thing I will never be in is a threesome, let alone an orgy. It's just really uncomfortable for me. It feels disingenuous to me. It could work for other people but for me, it just shows how greedy the person you're with is. Now, a threesome could work if you've been with someone for years and you've built and established a foundation and there's no question about who's going anywhere. But I'm just not there yet.

This situation just reminded me of how sacred sex is to me. It is not an act of just getting one off for me, it's deeper than that. If I give you my body, it's because I care about you. It's because I have feelings for you. It's not because I just want to have sex. It also made me realize that a lot of people are just out here having sex, especially in the gay community. It made me pay attention and open my eyes to who I'm talking to, dating, and any signs early on of what the situation is at its core.

I don't want to play the victim and say "Oh my

God, they took advantage of me," because obviously at any moment I could've gotten up to leave. I do want to take accountability for what I did. It's just that I've never experienced anything like that or been put on the spot like that and it almost felt like peer pressure.

It just taught me to be grounded in my boundaries and what I want in a partner. At the time, I did it to please my "partner," but all in all...all it did was fuck me up.

Please yourself.

Learning & Healing from Sexual Mishaps

Chapter Three:
Who Goes There!

So I have this ex...who's not necessarily an ex, more like one of those "situationships" you could say. We met years ago in high school when I used to cheer for Middle River Rec and he was on the football team. His name was Robbie and we were in a relationship for a little bit, but you know how in high school guys try to play with you and paint this picture like "That's not my girl, we just fucking?" Yeah...we were really in a relationship for about six or seven months but whatever. I just let him think what he wanted to think.

I used to get my friend Derek to drive me to Essex, MD to go see him often. The sex was amazing. It was great because we were young then. We had no idea what *real* sex even meant so it made fucking fun and took some of the pressure off. I trusted him as far as giving him my body and everything that came with it.

There was one time I was at his house and my stepdad was supposed to pick me up this time instead of Derek. It was the middle of winter, around 5 PM, so it was fairly early when I got dropped off but it got dark out much faster. It was also a weekday so my stepdad got off work around 6 PM and was scheduled to get me around 7 PM. Thank God, because Robbie was acting very weird.

You know how when you're young you don't have time in between after school and parents coming home to play around? Well, we got right into it. He was standing up and I was on the bed lying on my back with my legs in the air. Everything felt amazing but he just kept looking behind him. Then he turned back to me with a smirk on his face. I'm looking like "What are you looking at? What are you looking at?" He made it very obvious that something wasn't right. We had sex before and it was never like this.

Normally I would put a blanket on top of us until we got going because I'm always cold. But this time he didn't want me to put the blanket on, which was a little weird to me because I always did. That triggered something in my mind for sure, but I didn't think anything of it because I didn't think he would ever try to exploit me in any way. So I just ignored it. I thought maybe he just wanted to get right into it since we didn't have much time together. There weren't any moans or anything from what I can remember. It was pretty quiet. There was no TV on and the lights were off, except for the glowing light radiating the room from something on his nightstand.

All of a sudden rustling noises started coming from the closet. At this point, I'm like "Stop playing with me!" because I was scared.
Like who the hell is in the closet? Are they recording us? What are they doing? Turns out they never recorded us, they were just watching. It was creepy. At that point, I broke up with him on the spot. I didn't trust him anymore.

As I was waiting for my stepdad to come get me, he was out on his back patio trying to talk to other females! So I'm like okay so this is what we're doing? He even made it seem like it was my fault. Asking me why am I acting this way and why am I leaving. It was super uncomfortable.

I've never had someone literally, not even record because we weren't being recorded by that person, and I've recorded sex with a partner with my consent of course, say "Oh I have a guy in the closet." I never got an explanation for it. It's like an unsolved mystery. Why was he in the closet? More importantly, who was in the closet? I never even saw the guy. I know it was one of his friends, I'm just not sure which one. He came out and ran straight downstairs. I didn't see him at all. It was fucking weird. It makes you think about how many times it did happen and he got away with it. It also could've happened multiple times with different people, but maybe that particular person couldn't hold himself together. You never know.

    It wasn't a long relationship so not that if he would've told me it would've made a difference, because it would've been a no, but why would you do that to me? We were cool. It was nothing crazy. He didn't cheat on me or anything. He was a nonchalant, chill, laid-back type of guy. He wasn't a bad person or rude. He was coming off as really respectful. It was just one of those situations where it's like oh he's kind of a good guy and then he pulls some stuff like this. Like what are you doing? Why do you want to show your friends my body or what we do in the bedroom? That's weird to me. And did you come up with this or did your friend come up with this? How did this come about? Were you *really* a good guy? I feel like sex kind of shows you a different view of somebody.

    It was crazy. After that situation, I couldn't trust anybody for a while. I couldn't trust them with my body. I couldn't trust being in the house with anybody. I didn't trust anything. It took me about a year to get comfortable with someone again. I would talk to guys on the phone, we would text, but I wouldn't send any nudes or have sex with anyone. I didn't hang out with anybody outside of school unless we were close friends at that point because I just didn't trust anybody. Men in general. This person put me through this so what makes you think the next man wouldn't? This guy told me how loved me! You love me but you would exploit me like that?

Now, it's normal to have people watching you sexually with Onlyfans and things like that but back then we weren't into that so it was really scary. What if it went totally left and he and his friend held me down and took advantage of me? Although it was traumatizing and I never told anyone, I did forgive him eventually. We spoke very casually but we never got back together or anything because he should've never put me in that situation. You just can't come back from that.

Now that I'm older, I have to be somewhere with someone I'm having sex with where I can see everything. If I'm not at my house I'm definitely looking around. It just put me in a position where I'm more skeptical and aware of my surroundings. I examine everything.

I'm looking around like who's in here? Who's home?
Who can hear us? Who can see us? You know how at first when you go to your man's house you jump right into it? No, no, no. We're going to sit here for a little bit and I'm going to look around to make sure that nobody else is in this house.

This can happen to anyone. You just have to be careful and mindful that the person you're giving your body to you can trust wholeheartedly. But the thing is...I did and it backfired on me.

Certain things you just shouldn't take outside of the bedroom.

Learning & Healing from Sexual Mishaps

Chapter Four:
Where Do I Stick It?

I was around 12 years old. Old enough to know what sex was but not old enough to have any sexual experiences...to me at least. I was someone who got my period late. I don't want to say I was exposed to sex early but I knew what it was without knowing what it was. For instance, I've seen my older guy cousins watch porn when I was young, so I knew what it was, but I didn't know where everything went or the intricacies of it.

So there was this guy that I always played with at my aunt's house. He was about a year older than me. We would play outside together. I was a real tomboy back then who rode bikes and everything, so we hung out a lot when he would come over. So one night he was staying over with us. We did it all the time so it wasn't a big thing.

Next thing I knew, he flips on porn and I'm like "What the fuck? We're at my aunt's house! What are you doing?" He's like "You wanna do what they're doing?" and I'm like "No. What are you talking about?" But he's insistent. He's like "Come on let's try it!" and I'm like "Nah." It was during that time when they had porn on TV. Where you had to go all the way up in the channels to HBO or Cinemax. He's flicking through the channels trying to find something else so I'm like "I'm going to the bathroom." I go to the bathroom and in my mind, I'm like "Man this boy is tripping. I'm not with none of this or nothing like that." Mind you, I did like him but still, I wasn't with none of that.

I ended up coming back out to the living room and I'm like okay, I'm going to just tell him no. So I come back out there and he's already butterball naked! I'm like "What are you doing!" and he's like "Come on, let's try it" and saying whatever he can to convince me. I finally caved and said "Okay," I pulled my pants down. But this is how you know we were young and had no idea what we were doing. He goes "Alright...alright, where do I stick it?" I'm like "You don't even know what you're doing?"

So he's literally about to put it in my asshole...and my aunt bursts in like "What y'all doing!" So he's hastily trying to hurry up and get dressed as I'm trying to get myself together too. It was a mess. It was like she knew what was going on. It was one of the craziest moments of my life but I'm so thankful that she burst through that door because obviously, I didn't know what I was doing, and neither did he. Trying to be grown, watching what's on the TV.

I'll never forget what she said.
She sat me down, and she's like "Look, I don't know what you were doing but I know you didn't want to do it. Don't let nobody make you do nothing that you don't want to do." I was happy to have that conversation with her. To be able to say "You know I didn't want to do it but it was a pressure type of thing." And she's like "Yeah, you lucky I came in." We kind of laughed about the situation.

It was awkward after that situation to see him because he was not allowed over anymore rightfully so. We just stopped playing all together and went our separate ways. We never talked about it after either. I saw him around because we had the same group of friends but we never discussed it. When I did see him we were mostly outside. We were never sitting in the same room alone.

I didn't tell anyone else because of my lack of knowledge. I thought I knew about sex, but clearly, I didn't know enough. So for me to go around telling people who were experienced about my lack of experience just made me feel embarrassed.

I think that moment traumatized me because I didn't end up losing my virginity until a lot later than other people did. I think that had a lot to do with it. It was a combination of things. Getting caught of course and then not knowing. And you know the sex ed classes don't really teach you. It's like they teach you, but not enough. It definitely shook me up. After that, it was just one of those things where I'm like "Nah, I'm good." I kind of felt like I didn't have a choice in the matter. It was pressure and the result was embarrassment for both of us.

People do put pressure on but I'm not one to give in to pressure too much in any experience.

Subconsciously, I think that plays a part in it.

Chapter Five:
A Delicate Flower

So when I had my daughter in October, I gave birth to her alone because her father was locked up at the time. Me dealing with having a baby by myself, then having another small child that isn't too far apart in age, and him coming home two months after my daughter was born...was an experience. He was locked up for months, so he hadn't had sex in months.

When he comes home, a few weeks before Christmas, he's like "Oh the baby, the baby...SEX" and I'm like "Umm, I'm not ready for that." There was so much that I was going through emotionally and physically. It was my second C-section and I feel like I healed a lot differently.

I healed quicker with the second, but with the first one, it was a completely different experience. So he comes home and he's like yes, sex. I'm like okay I had an infant and a toddler at the time, which was difficult. I don't know how I was even able to let this happen. But he's like "Okay, so we're going to put the baby to sleep and do this." It's just me and him. I'm telling him "Just ease it into me." I'm explaining to him that this is like the first time all over again because I remember what it was like to have sex again after I had my son. I feel like this every time I have a child and I think associating sex with that feeling is why I wasn't necessarily ready. So that was on my mind and also I've been away from him longer than ever before. I knew he had all that testosterone built up in him.

A Delicate Flower

I just felt like I wasn't sure if I was really prepared for it. I was scared that we were going to start and he was going to be animalistic. I just wasn't in that mindset. I felt like a delicate flower.

So we did...and I kind of wish I would've waited.

He reassured me that he would be delicate and gentle. Which kind of didn't happen. He attempted to in the beginning for sure. And I just felt like a switch went off at one point and I had to tell him like "Look, you need to get off. You need to get off!" He's just like "Oh, I'm sorry." But I just knew it was too much. He tried to hear me out. He tried his best to hear me out when I explained that to him. He was concerned about my feelings but he just also went through something that was kind of traumatizing to him too, so I think it was hard for him to process how I felt because of how he felt himself. I wouldn't say I only needed the time to heal myself after having a baby, I would say he needed the time to heal himself too. We both, going through life changes so abruptly, should've just taken time to preserve ourselves and be more sound, and together. So that when we did, it would be like fireworks.

I felt like I should've listened to myself and listened to my body because it was not pleasurable to me at all. It was miserable to be very honest. But because I'm trying to be mindful of him, my man at the time, and what he was just going through, I kind of put my feelings of what I was going through in my own body after him. I wish I wouldn't have done that. I would tell women, especially women who have maybe dealt with situations like that, to just do it when you're ready. Because what's the point of having sex if you're not enjoying it?

Or if your body is just not ready? Your body is doing all these things to tell you like "Hey you're not ready yet, just calm down." But me trying to be a good partner and understanding of my partner, it's like I forced myself to kind of suffer in silence. Now looking back on it I wish I would've been more vocal about not being ready for it and maybe we could've handled it a different way. I was already mad at the facts of the situation. That he was gone for so long and I already had a baby by myself. I could've tended to myself so much better emotionally before just jumping right into having sex. It was just so much. The baby, him coming home from jail, and me feeling this way. He had all this energy built up. Anger or whatever was going on with him. Now we're transferring this energy. It was too much.

    I was also healing from my insecurities about my C-section scar. My first C-section was done by a woman and how it was sewn was perfect. I would wear bathing suits and feel totally confident. But my second one was done by a man and he sewed my stomach unevenly. I'm very insecure about it. So then dealing with the insecurities of feeling like I'm not attractive while having sex, it was just so many things going on at that time. I was not in the right headspace. What worked for me was communicating that to my partner. I'm like look, I don't feel as attractive as before you went away.

    He would do things to reassure me that he was still attracted to me, he still loved me, and he was grateful that I had his kids. But I could've advocated for myself more. Be very vocal and don't suffer in silence, especially when you have a partner willing to hear you out and you're supposed to be going through life together. That was a big thing for me. I feel like in our culture especially, women are told to "calm down," or we're "doing the most" when we face an issue because we're deemed overly emotional when we're not acting like everything is okay. But the truth of the matter is… Everything is not always okay. Sometimes I'm not okay. Sometimes I'm emotional and sometimes I want to cry it out. I feel like that being a normal thing for women and men would be beneficial to partnerships and families as a whole. Because you need to be your best self to be with your partner, so when you come together you're the best for your children. Time, communication, and effort are the biggest factors in avoiding things like this.

Giving yourself more time after you're pregnant to have somebody, even if it is your partner, introduce themselves to your body again is important. We go through a lot of changes during and after pregnancy and every pregnancy is so different.

I would say to give yourself more time, be patient, and don't let anyone peer pressure you. Also, don't allow the guilt of your partner or how they're handling things, to pressure you into a decision that might not be beneficial to you.

Be vocal. Don't suffer in silence.
Accidents do happen all the time, but some things can be avoided.

Chapter Six:
Up In Arms

So there was this guy James that I used to work with. I think we met in 2013. We were always cool. We always had a good friendship and a nice bond at work. I never wanted to do it with him or anything like that. It wasn't until after I left that job that we started to flirt, gained a connection, and started having sex. Usually, our sneaky links happened in the car or somewhere like that. Little lunch break sessions or quickies in the car before we headed back to work. It was never in a room.

The first time we got a room at the Quality INN, we went to the bar to drink beforehand. So we were drunk and high when we got back to the hotel room. We were excited like "Yes! We have all this room now. We can do what we want to do. We're going to fuck on the counters, on everything! We're going to tear this place up and leave."

So we get there and we're having fun. He ran down to the front desk for something, and I was back in the room getting ready. I'm hyping myself up like "Bitch it's your time to shine! It's time to put it on this man!" He walks in the door and I barely have any clothes on besides my bra. He looked at me like he wanted to fucking devour me, so I'm like alright, let's get it in.

We started kissing and heading to the bed. When we get to the bed, I sit down to pull his dick out while he's getting undressed. I love to give head so I'm sitting there excited and ready. I started sucking his dick leaning back on the bed, propping myself up with my arms while he was standing in front of me. He's fucking my throat but he's doing it to the point where he's still respecting my boundaries. I told him "Look, if you're going to do it then don't do it too hard. We can both meet the goal if you don't do it too hard." So he starts getting into it. He's moaning. I'm pleasing him. We're in a nice little groove and motion. Everything is fine...and then all of a sudden my arm slips while he's going in at the same time. So his whole ten-and-a-half-inch dick goes all the way down my throat!

I instantly started throwing up all over the place. Mind you, we went to eat before then. I had pasta and some more shit. So I got broccoli all over this man's dick. It's bad! I'm like what. the. fuck. In my head, I was still drunk so I was still trying to finish. He's like "Babe don't worry about it. It's all good" and I'm like "No it's not!"

So at this point, we're in a mix of emotions. I don't know if we should keep going or should we not. I got pasta and fettuccine all over this sexy ass man...and this is our first time in a hotel room, I'm about to give him the business, and we just fuck it all the way up. He ended up going to the shower and cleaning off his dick and everything.

We did end up having sex but the entire time we're doing it I'm just like "Yo, my throat hurts." I even made him hit it from the back because I didn't want him to see me at that moment, let alone see me in pain. I still wanted to get him to where he wanted to be and make him cum but I was hurting. I stuck it out like a trooper, but he saw it in my face afterward and heard it. It was so raspy instantly. I couldn't even moan for him the way that he wanted me to. We were just trying to get through it.

Afterward, of course, he asked me if I was okay but eventually, I finally said "No, I'm not.

I can't even fake it anymore." I know it wasn't my fault. I mean yeah, I slipped so I know it wasn't his fault either. I was trying to reassure him the entire time by patting him on his shoulder, rubbing his head, and playing with his beard. Still trying to be sexy with no voice. He felt so bad.

For the rest of that evening, I couldn't swallow. I couldn't do anything. I was dumbfounded. I never had anything like this happen to me before. Still, to this day, it was the worst experience I've had. I think I've told only one other person about this. That shit really fucked me up. To the point where he tries to hit me up now to come and see me and stuff like that but I keep bluffing him. I automatically start thinking back to that time. On top of being embarrassing, it was painful as hell. For two days everybody thought I was sick or something. I didn't have a voice. I couldn't swallow or eat or anything. Even when I tried to drink something, it was the worst, sore, raw feeling in the world.

I called my doctor on the second day. She didn't laugh at me initially, but once we started talking about it she giggled a little bit. I tried explaining to her through my raspy voice that my throat was sore and swollen, I was sucking on cough drops, and using the throat spray to numb it. She just told me that it would have to heal on its own. I could continue with the throat lozenges to give it that cool effect and drink liquids to help soothe it. Drinks like honey tea with lemon would make the inflammation and soreness go down and everything would be okay. But if I went a week without talking and I didn't have a voice, then we would have to talk again because I definitely messed something up.

So then I was sitting there freaking out like wow, I gotta go through all of this.

But I am glad that it was him that I experienced it with. We've always had a good relationship as far as being open and talking about anything, especially when it comes to sex. We've always discussed limits, boundaries, and everything of that nature. We respected each other's bodies, so when it came down to this situation he felt really bad. He said things like "I just want to hold you. Do you need me to get you some ice cream?" But I couldn't swallow or anything. It was a lot.

    It took me 2-3 days to heal physically. I vividly remember my mom making dinner that following Sunday. It was all the good stuff but I couldn't eat any of it. I had to sit there and act like I could because I couldn't tell my mom "Hey, I just had a dick shoved down my throat so I can't really eat right now." I had to sit there and at least try to enjoy it but it took me a few days to even feel like I could eat again. It took around five days altogether to feel like there was no more soreness or irritation.

    Mentally...I'm still shaken by it because I won't even meet up with this man again. We did this in 2017, so it's been about 3-4 years. He even hit me up recently and I'm texting back, flirting, and all that but when it comes to physically meeting with him...I'm scared. I need my throat and my mind to fully recover from this. As I've said, we've always been open and honest with one another, so I decided to just get out of my head and talk to him.

    The last time I spoke to him, I let him know by saying "Listen, I'm not going to lie to you, I'm having a hard time recovering from our last rendezvous, mentally more than anything. I want to get back with you and do stuff again but I'm real life traumatized, not purposefully, by what happened." He said it could sense that from me and he somewhat laid into me like, "Why didn't you just tell me? We talk about everything." But now that he could understand where I was coming from, he let me know to do it in my own time. Of course, we still sext and Facetime each other, but we said we would take seeing each other and having sex again slowly, on my time, and when I'm ready.

    As a woman who loves giving head, yeah I'll give it still, but now I give it differently. I'll never be in a situation where I'm physically in that position ever again. Giving head after that I was scared as shit. I thought, let me try with a man that's smaller than what he was just in case. I tried dotting all of my I's and crossing my T's first. It took me a minute to get with somebody else after him. I didn't want to have sex. I didn't want to suck any dick. I didn't want to be a part of anything. But I am someone who enjoys it, so when I first got back into it I had to work my way back up. It still messes with my mind now a little bit. But now I just make sure I'm not in that position. If I'm tipsy or anything like that, I'm being more mindful of what I'm doing. At first, it did ruin sexual experiences for me because I am so spontaneous, impulsive, and all the good stuff mixed. I was overcalculating how to please somebody. Now I'm like just get out of your head.

    If you find yourself in a situation like this, reach out to somebody. Don't guilt yourself or your partner, especially if it was accidental. It's okay. In that moment everything feels like it's turning upside down because it's something that you're not used to and didn't expect. Usually, when people experience trauma, it's somebody who means to hurt them but this is a different scenario. It's harder to cope with your emotions, as far as not looking at that person and saying they hurt me, rather than taking a minute to process it and realizing it wasn't intentional.

Take a moment to step back from the situation to analyze it. Don't beat yourself up over it. Or tell someone else about it that you trust, that you love, or you know cares for you. When I spoke to my best friend about it, getting it off my chest made me feel so much better. She even ended up sharing one of her traumatic stories with me as well, so it made me feel at ease. It's nothing to be completely embarrassed about. It happens. Not specifically this situation but accidental sexual experiences happen. It's more about how you cope and move forward with it that really counts.

Be patient with yourself. No healing process is overnight.

Chapter Seven:
Older, And None The Wiser

It's pretty traumatizing dealing with older men. I started dealing with an older man sexually when I was about 18 and he was 31. I'm thinking "Ooo, this is where it's at," but in reality...no it wasn't. They are way more advanced than what we need. They know mind games and things like that, that we don't know then. Having a traumatic experience as a child where I was molested by one of my mom's friends, and not having her believe me until one of her other friends spoke up, and then dealing with men like that as I got older, birthed a sort of pattern for me.

    I used to dance, so I would date a lot of guys that were older than me anyway. But the first guy that I dealt with sexually was 31. His name was Hassan and I met him at the strip club. I thought he was sweeping me off my feet. He had all this money and the lavish lifestyle that I wanted. So I thought okay, this is what I'm going to go after. Then it all just ended up falling right on me. Everything that he portrayed himself to be was the total opposite but I believed it because that was the potential I saw in him. I'm like okay, well...he could be this or he could be that, but in reality, he wasn't necessarily anything. It took me about six years to realize it wasn't really what I thought.

    I met him through a girl who was having sex with him at the club I was working at. She's like "Girl, let's go over there, have some crabs. Blah, blah, blah." We went over there to eat and he kept coming back and forth to the club after that. He found out I liked to clean. I love cleaning. That's what I do. So I would come and clean this big ass house and he would pay me $700 every time I would do it. I'm thinking "Oh okay that's some money so let me see what else he has going on." But that money that he would get from people would be like stolen money. It was always money that he was supposed to do something else with and he would just spend it all. He was essentially a scammer. He scammed me and that's how he got me. He saw that I was making money and I saw that he was making money. He was like "Hey if you give me $20,000, I'll give you $40,000." That's exactly what he said to me. You give me this and I'll give you that. It sounded like a dream. Do you think I've ever seen that? I've never seen that. I did live in a place with him for a while and he claims that with the rent and all the weed that I smoked and this and that, it added up to $20,000.

I dealt with him when I was 18, up until I was 26. I went back to him, even after he did all that with my money. For whatever reason I still felt like let me see something else...maybe he changed. But he didn't change at all.

Sex played a big factor in that. He was very sexual. That's how our relationship even started. I didn't think he was cute. It wasn't until we had sex and I came for the first time that I was like "Woah, this is some real shit." So from there, it was kind of like manipulation through sex because that's what he liked to do obviously. Manipulate and scam people.

He lived with his baby's mom. He was having sex with me and I guess having sex with her. He was even having sex with my friend before he knew me, so I had no idea who he was having sex with at that point.

No idea. I just know I never got anything.

He used sex to dominate me until he couldn't anymore because there was a point in time when I was just completely turned off. I noticed what he was doing. I realized that there wasn't anything else that was attractive besides sex. We couldn't hold a conversation. I'm just looking at him like why are we on Facetime? I want to hang up. It was one of those things. So I just had to realize, like okay, maybe I need to move on and that's what I did. But it took me having two abortions. The first one was really bad and I told myself I was done dealing with him and I didn't want to have sex with him anymore. But I wound up still having sex with him and then I had the second abortion which was horrible. He didn't speak to me afterward. He told me that he didn't mind me having a baby but also asked if I was sure it wasn't anyone else's. He accused me of a few things. It was really bad and that's what made me say let me get the fuck away from him. He was 37 by the way. Ten years my senior with kids from previous relationships already. I knew it was time to get away.

I met one of his baby's moms and I could just see her demeanor. You could see pictures from back when they were together and she just looked so bad, versus how she looks now. She just looks so happy and lively now. Like she actually wants to be a person. I could see myself turning into that. I could see my skin fading. I wasn't as happy as I should've beeen.

I wasn't even really in my family's life like that. He would kind of shut me out of everything. He was very manipulative. He was a narcissist I've come to find out. Once I pulled his card and told him who he was, from there he tried to discard me. I was this and that, having sex with other people, but I said whatever it's not even worth it. It was really bad. I never really had a chance to tell him that I was done. It showed in my actions.

This past year, I had a birthday party. He came and met my family and everything. But it wasn't like "Hey guys! This is my boyfriend. This is…" He felt some type of way but he's never introduced me like that. It was my birthday! I was having a good time in the company of my friends and family and he just came. So I introduced him and that was that but I guess I was hanging with my friends too much because that night he went through my phone. He woke me up around 3:30 in the morning and cussed me out. He told me I should've let him know that I wasn't serious and this and that. I'm just sitting there thinking "Why are you going through my phone?" If you're looking for something…in reality you're going to find something. He was doing something. He was always doing something, so he just wanted to find a reason to make him seem like the victim. From there it was just downhill. He would want me to check in with him and call him but I wasn't even doing shit! So my actions just started to show that I wasn't feeling it anymore.

That was a lesson to be learned and I had to learn it. I have gone through life searching for love in different kinds of ways, and I felt like since he was older he would be able to give it to me. Like since he was older he should know what to do and the right way to do it but no. There's no book on this. You learn how you learn through the examples that you're given and he wasn't giving too many good examples. I wasn't either.

I was just hoping that he was going to help me figure it out but he didn't and ultimately it put me right back in the same place where I was in the beginning. I should've just avoided him altogether but I saw something that wasn't there because he was older.

I wouldn't always say to avoid older men but use your mind over your heart. I can go back to every situation that has turned bad and say that there was something that told me to go before I actually did. We don't listen to ourselves. We listen to songs or whatever but no.

Listen to yourself because it's giving you a plain example right there.

That's the easiest advice I could give.

Chapter Eight:
Blown

I had this old coworker Rodney. I used to work at Amazon and there was this guy I guess you would call my supervisor or whatever. He always showed me all this attention and that he liked me, but he was a little nerdy, and he seemed like he was a little "slow." But for some reason, I was still attracted to him and I was just like you know what? Alright.

After months and months, and months of him asking to hang out and all that stuff I'm like okay let me see what he's about. It was random how I ended up at his house that night, but one night I went to the movies with someone else, and that guy made me upset. He made me so upset because he came late and I feel like he came late on purpose because he didn't want to pay for the movie.

I ended up paying for the movie, going in first, then he met me there. But it was the most boring date I have ever fucking been on. It fucking made me so upset. After that, I'm like okay what am I going to do? Because by this time I was living downtown, I was at the Charles Theater, and I was like should I walk home or should I go do something else?

So I just randomly texted Rodney and asked him what he was doing. He said he was cooking and invited me over. So I went over and when I got to the apartment, (he lives near me) it was cool or whatever. It was a nice little setup. But you know some of the apartments in the city are old on the inside as far as appliances and things.

He didn't have a microwave. It was kind of like a stove sat by itself and the kitchen was weird. He cooked some baked chicken with peppers or something on top, and I forgot what the side dish was, but it wasn't that good. I was just like oh okay, whatever. He fed me and he tried.

Then, we were chilling and watching TV. I think we were watching YOU on Netflix. Things started to get a little hot, and risky, and all of that. We were kissing and he was fingering me and all that other good stuff. I think I stayed the night that night so we decided to take things to the bedroom. Before we did that, he left...Mind you it was like midnight when we started getting sexual and he decided to leave and go to the gas station! He's like "I got to go, I got to step out real quick."

So I'm like alright, okay...He was out there for about 30 to 45 minutes and I thought the gas station was right around the corner on St.Paul st so what are you doing? I thought about it more like...is this motherfucker getting crack? He's either getting crack, weed, or a gas station pill. Now I'm just like okay...and when he comes back he's just like "Okay I'm ready." And I'm like wait, wait, wait, what did you leave for? He says, "You know it's been a long time…" He went on to tell me it's been 10 years since he's been in a real relationship and all of that. Cool.

So once he officially came back in, we got to having sex or whatever. The first thing I noticed that was weird was he would not let me give him oral sex. When he mentioned the reason why I was like oh okay, you get a pass. He said, "You know, I'd rather do that with my girlfriend." So we didn't do oral at all. We started having sex but he had a big ass fan in the window and you know sometimes when the air is circulating in the area, you might dry out. So he has the fan blowing on me directly and I'm just like okay...I started drying up. So then he gets the lube. Shibari lube. I saw it a lot at Amazon so I was pretty sure he got it from there. Poured it on my coochie. Poured it! And starts ramming himself inside of me. In my head, I'm like I know I'm going to have BV when this is done. Lo and behold, the next day I'm like I feel weird, I smell weird, and I know what BV is like because I had it before. I'm just thinking this nigga is stupid! I was so pissed when I went to the doctor and I had BV. Like, bitch, why would you put all of that lubricant on me? You didn't need it. You just needed to turn the fan off. I kept telling him that.

We only had sex that one time. I cut him off.

I feel like when you really don't want to pursue somebody...just don't. Because I felt like that situation could've been avoided with Rodney. Even though I was attracted to him and kind of wanted to date and see what it was about, at the same time, a lot of my subconscious was like bitch no. What are you doing? You're not that desperate.

When you feel like your intuition is telling you no don't fucking do it, don't do it.

Sexidents

Chapter Nine:
I Know You're Single Bitch But...

So about this dude named Dre...we've known each other for a couple of years because when I used to blog and everything, he used to show his support. When I started doing photography, he was doing the same thing, but we really only knew each other from social media until he started Ubering. A couple of times he's come and taken me to the market and all of that, so he's been to my house, but we never did anything. We would always converse over Facebook Messenger and talk about what we would do with each other if we ever fucked or whatever. He would send me pictures of his dick and I would send him pictures too. We kept that going for a long time.

But one day, I was feeling really horny and I was just like "I wanna give you a hand job, a massage, or whatever." I already kind of knew what it would turn into but I still was like okay, let me see. I'm like bitch, this is only supposed to be a hand job. Don't be going and sucking and fucking no dick or nothing! When he got there, I had set the mood and everything. I made it a cute little night. I lit some incense, put some music on, took a shower, and put on my silk robe. I didn't have anything under it. I smelled amazing. I made the night really cute!

He comes over. First of all...I had to take his hat off because his fucking hairline was receding! When I tell you this nigga slept with this fitted on...he slept with his fitted on but I digress.

It was a little bit of small talk before shit got started. He brought this big ass jar of coconut oil. For starters, it looked like a jar he uses as his everyday moisturizer for his body. It was hard! He brought it over and didn't even melt it, or soften it, or nothing. We had to put that shit in the microwave. I knew it was something he used every day because it had hair and shit in it. I was just like alright, whatever. I warmed up the coconut oil, he laid on the bed and pulled his dick out so I started massaging it and everything. Then I started sucking it! Because I was just kind of in the groove so I'm like okay let's give him the double treatment or whatever.

After a while, we got undressed and started having sex. We did not use a condom and I don't know why but the sex was great! It was amazing. Even with the fitted cap on it was amazing. We had sex so many times that night.

But the kicker was when the morning came and I could see everything in the apartment...I turned over at him and he's just knocked out in my bed with the fitted on. Like are you serious? And then I look at his skin. Peeling. Like really bad. I was just staring at him and I'm like you know your skin is peeling a little bit? He was just like "Yeah, I got real dry skin." But I'm looking at the flakes on my bed and I'm upset. Like, ew. Then I asked him straight up "Why won't you take your hat off? He's like "Because yo, my shit not cut and I usually keep it bald." I could see hair coming out the back so I knew he probably had the George Jefferson going on. I'm thinking like okay, that's peculiar. You just slept in my bed the whole night with a whole fitted on but whatever. Add that to the peeling skin shit and it was just irritating. He just looked bad! His skin was all fucked up in the face. He looked really old. He just looked bad to me.

I got dressed. He got dressed. I had to work that day so he took me to work. We stopped at McDonalds to get food or whatever.

Mind you, this guy was acting like a fan. He just kept saying " I never thought I would be here. I've been watching you for a long time." He really sounded like a fan. I'm just like okay, whatever. I don't pay shit like that no mind. I couldn't care any less.

But, the next day I woke up, had to urinate, and I thought I had a UTI. You know that uncomfortable feeling when you pee and the pressure that comes right after? So I thought "Oh my God I have a UTI." I did remember peeing after I had sex and drinking a lot of water, so how did I get a UTI? So I took my ass to Patient First, told them my symptoms, and then I said I think I have a UTI. Then I told them I would like to be tested too. They tested me and it came back...and this nigga had Trichomoniasis and gave it to me. I don't think he knew he had it because men don't get symptoms for it. He definitely didn't say anything about his dick feeling any type of way. So I chucked it up to him not experiencing any symptoms. When the test results came back, I was just fucking humiliated. I felt dirty. I felt crazy. Even though it was an STI, and not something even more life threatning, I still felt fucking crazy although I did not transmit the disease.

When I called my doctor, they said "You should notify your last sexual partners." It felt bizarre, but I reached out to him and then the person I had sex with before. The person I had sex with before said "I got tested after I had sex with you and I was good." So I immediately thought it could only be one person. I reached out to him and told him what was up. I was like "Yo, I have Trichomoniasis and I reached out to the last two people

I Know You're Single Bitch But...

I had sex with and the other person didn't have it so you need to go get checked out." I was grateful that they both were mature about it and didn't go off and shit. It was more like okay, I'll take care of this. Dre was very much embarrassed. He said things like "I'm really embarrassed by this. I'm just so sorry," blah, blah, blah. Eventually, he got tested and he did have it. He said, "I probably got it from the woman I had sex with before you or whatever." But it's like if I was really crazy I would've beat your ass! For real. That's somebody's health you're playing with. It opened my eyes. I already thought men might have the cooties all the time. But now, that's what I automatically assume. That's just how I think. This was the biggest wake-up call. Like bitch you cannot just be having sex with niggas. I know you're single bitch but slow the fuck down.

Now, I can tell he's trying to overcompensate for what happened between us because now he's just supporting any damn thing that I do. I could fucking go outside and piss on the ground and he'll be like "Yooo I like that! It's cool! I fuck with that." He's definitely overcompensating because he did that to me and he probably thinks I told people. I think he's probably telling the truth about where he got it from and all of that. He doesn't come off as that type of person that would lie but you can't put shit past anybody. Who knows...

I'm just grateful it was something that could be cleared up and I went on my way. He was like you probably never want to have sex with me again. You are damn right! Do you think I'm going to have sex with you ever again? That's dead. Because that means you not taking care of your shit after you fuck with people.

The moral of the story is to get tested and keep up with getting tested. Just be careful. Don't trust everybody with your body. They could easily not be taking care of themselves. You know how men are like "Oh she got tested so I'm fine," and leave it at that? I don't want any of my friends to have to experience that, or my little sisters.

Go get tested.

Learning & Healing from Sexual Mishaps

Chapter Ten:
Who Pulls The Strings?

I was dating this guy, he was a Taurus, and he was very sexual. We would do all kinds of stuff together. We met online. This was in the era of Black Planet and all of that. I would say we dated, not seriously, for almost a year. He was basically like my fuck buddy. If I wasn't dealing with anybody or whatever, I could call him. I would go over there, we would hook up, and it was always great and exciting. But it didn't last because he was very open. A little too open honestly. I was okay with it for a short while but after some time, I wanted something more committed, not just sex. I also didn't want to be married at that time either, so until I got clear on what I truly wanted, I had to call it quits. We stayed friends for a while. We would keep in touch, checking up on each other occasionally because we did have a deep connection when we were dating. But at the end of the day, I said to myself I can't keep doing this. I need something more solid. We were really good friends and we didn't have sex for a while. But naturally I caved and we eventually rekindled our flame. And then, we were probably having sex for about six months or so, not even a year when this happened.

It was a typical link for us. Except this time when I went to his house, I told him I was on my period, so he didn't expect us to have sex as we normally did. I had never experienced sex on my period before. Hadn't even thought about it because most guys are always like "Ew, periods, gross!" They won't even pick up tampons from the store out of embarrassment. As if buying tampons will automatically turn them into women. I thought he would be so turned off that it would result in a nice, chill night together without all the bells and whistles. But boy was I in for a surprise.

We started messing around. Kissing and grabbing one another. In the middle of our makeout session, he asked me straightforwardly, "You have a tampon in?" and nervously, I responded, "Yeah I do," not thinking too deep into it. "Okay whatever..." he dryly said, so I thought that was the end of the conversation. Little did I know that when he got up, he would be bringing back a towel with him. He laid it down on the bed next to me. Like I said, I had never experienced this before so I didn't know what he was doing. Amid our passionate makeout session, my pants came off. I should've known what was coming next given the question and the fact that I was pantsless but nothing could prepare me for what I was due to experience.

He gently puts the towel down, slightly opens my legs, grabs the string of my tampon, and yanks it out of my vagina! He just whipped it out like it wasn't even there and mentally I freaked out! I froze.

He nonchalantly shrugged, "Whatever, I don't care," and continued as if nothing ever happened. He genuinely did not care that I was on my period. I could tell. Maybe he was just so horny that it didn't matter. But in my mind, I was screaming! I never heard of a man doing something like this. But I quickly learned in that moment that when men want to have sex, they'll do anything to get some. Even though the pull was an utter shock, he was surprisingly soft in the time after.

Who Pulls The Strings?

That was my first experience having sex on my period... and although it seemed absolutely insane at the time that he would pull my tampon out for me, the sex was actually better than I expected! It was amazing actually, but him doing that kind of made me like eh, what did I get myself into? There are certain things you just wouldn't tell anybody. I laugh now just thinking about it.

There are so many different types of people out here. I could've easily gone to the bathroom and taken it out privately if that's what he wanted. But I guess he just couldn't wait. Thinking back on it, there's no way he knew how to pull it so that it would come out so smoothly unless he's had practice. The way he did it so skillfully...he definitely had done it before.

Now, my current boyfriend and I usually have sex in the shower when I'm on my period. The shower is usually my go-to because you can just wash up after. It's just cleaner and easier that way. No towels or tampon removals. Very hygienic.

Just be aware of the people you meet, especially online. You never know what they're into.

Chapter Eleven:
Take It At Face Value

So when I got to college I wasn't very sexually experienced. When I went away to school I was 17, so I had my first real experiences when I got there.

I was dealing with this guy and most of the time we would just have sex but never any oral sex. I never had it, so there was no way to miss it, and I didn't feel the need to ask for it. But one time we were fooling around he's like "I'm going to give you head." I said, "Oh okay!" and because I never experienced it before, I thought if he was offering maybe it was time I finally tried it out. So, he goes down on me and I'm just like...Why is everybody so excited about this? I went to my best friend and I was like "Girl I had head for the first time and I don't get it. I don't understand."

She's like "What do you mean you don't understand? It's like the best thing in the world!" I quickly realized that he was just horrible at it. I didn't get anything out of it. I don't even think he did anything that had to do with the clit. It was like all on the outside, you know, everything but. I didn't get any type of orgasm. No enjoyable feeling. It was just wet and just there and I'm like okay...this is weird but this is what people are doing.

I never had an orgasm from oral sex until I got out of college, maybe about five years later... I dealt with people in between that time but it wasn't anything serious. Then I finally had *real* head and I called her up and I was like now I understand!

Because that first experience was nothing. Literally, nothing. People say this is what you do when you have sex, and I'm just letting him do it, thinking this is not doing anything the whole time because of it. I thought maybe I was one of those people who just didn't get an orgasm from oral. But after having another experience I realized that I didn't understand the process and I didn't understand my body enough to explain what I was looking for or how I should go about it. So I just took it as what it was. I never told him. I only told my best friend. We just kind of dated throughout college. I only attended that school for a year and it was probably roughly a semester that we were talking or whatever. So I never went back to explain or say anything afterward. I was just like this was strange...I'm just going to move on.

I think from that experience I kind of shied away from it when dealing with other people. I just didn't want to go through that experience with anyone else because it doesn't make any sense for it to not be enjoyable. I think that's why it was so long before I experienced it for real.

I also feel like I wasn't taught anything before having my experiences. I would kind of stay to myself. I didn't have experiences with guys here and there until I went to college. It was just like boom, I'm trying these things and I have no idea what I'm doing. I feel like there has to be someone teaching. Even if it's not a parent, maybe an older sibling, cousin, or friend depending on the age. Someone who has gone through the experiences to teach you about your body so that you know how to please it. I definitely didn't know my body back then. I learned it play-by-play through my sexual experiences. And to me, it wasn't the best way to do it. It would've been nice if I had known more about everything.

Maybe being able to masturbate and do things on my own so I know the feeling and what I'm looking to experience.

The only way to know what you like and don't like sexually is to know your body. Don't be afraid to explore it.

Chapter Twelve:
Lend Me Some Sugar

So I met this guy Mike...I was kind of interested in finding me a little sugar daddy because I was out on my own. So I found him on this site. It might have been Sugardaddy.com or something like that. He actually messaged me first. I can't remember what he said but when I saw his avatar he was just so fucking fine. You know I love me a bald head with a beard. I think he was 41 or 42 years old at that time. I was 21 but I've always been interested in older men.

    So we started talking and after a couple of days, he eventually wanted to meet up. So we met up and had dinner. Automatically the attraction was there. It was *there*. The attraction was so fucking deep that it didn't make any sense. I could look at this man and my panties get wet. It was just an instant sexual attraction. I mean, he was fine as fuck. And I mean obviously, he thought I was fine too. That night we had dinner, I was on my way home and he text me saying he pretty much wanted to fuck me so bad! I got home, he met me at my house that night, and we fucked. And let me just say his dick...was so fucking big. His dick was large. I loved it. The first time was absolutely amazing. And after that, we started to *really* get into the sex thing.

    But some other things were hard to ignore. Like the fact that I could never come to his house, or whenever I would call him he would never answer the phone, but he would text me. So I mean of course I started thinking... because initially he told me he was going through a separation and that his wife had left him for another man.

But eventually, I found out that this was all a lie.

    We would meet up probably like 2-3 times a week but we would only meet up at his job so we could fuck in the car. Typically it would go like this: we would meet up at a restaurant very close to his job, on his break or something like that, and then we would knock back a couple of drinks (I always got fucked up because that's the best way to have sex to be real with you,) and have mindblowing sex in the car. Mind you, the sex was always raw so it kind of got to the point where every time we had sex...throat babies. I'm not going to lie to you.
    It's wild to think that I knew so little about him. He was very secretive but it's something about a very mysterious person that just draws you…in. I was so drawn to him in the craziest ways. I would literally do anything this man asked. And thankfully, it wasn't much but sexually it was everything. It was mainly a sexual relationship.
    He would feed me bullshit basically and I just got so fucking sucked into it that it didn't make any sense. I mean what kind of dick does that to you? But I was 21, young, and just wanted some love. I truly desired love but I was drawn to toxicity, to be honest with you. Most of us with daddy issues are drawn to the most toxic men. We are drawn to older men and somehow drawn to married men. That's not my nigga, but somehow I'm in love with this man, and I don't even know he has a wife at home.
    So eventually I found out that the whole time that we were having all that sex, meeting up, getting drunk, fucking in public places...his wife was pregnant. He went away for a couple of days. You know, the typical three days that the mother is in the hospital.

He would lie and say "Oh my dad is in the hospital" or whatever. There were just so many fucking lies but somehow I believed the sad stories he would tell me about how his wife had left him for another man-type of deal. It was disgusting. It was truly disgusting. I don't even know what else to fucking say...but I was really on this man for about two years. Of course, he would tell me "We're trying to separate," or whatever the case may be. But then y'all have two kids and a business together. By the tail end of our relationship, he would tell me he's not leaving his wife because they have all of this shit together.

It hurt me to my core...but I still stayed.

I was so far gone. So far gone to the point where he controlled me in a sense. If he ever thought that I was messing with another guy...whenever he would come over I would delete certain texts from other guys, put my phone on vibrate, or cut it off just in case. It was like I didn't want to get in trouble. Like, I didn't want to give him a reason to stop fucking with me. He would blame me for shit, knowing damn well he was in the wrong, not me! You're not even my man! I'm talking to other guys! The dick had me doing shit that you would in a relationship. We even fucked in his house before. His wife was out of town and he invited me over.
A couple of weeks after that, we decided to break things off. I showed up at their house intending to tell his wife, but immediately realized that was dumb as hell. I simply put myself in a bad situation.
First of all, don't go just having sex with anybody. You really have to learn that person. You need to learn that person's habits. You need to learn that person's goods.

You need to learn that person's bads. Because you do not want to go into something and then you feel stuck. Those soul ties are super duper *real* because at the end of the day, sex is an exchange of energy. It's times when people will treat you so fucking bad, have you doing any and everything for them, because of that soul tie.

You do not want to put yourself in that situation because you are not in control anymore. I was gone off the dick many times, I'm not going to lie, but I learned my motherfucking lesson with this one.

Resources:

Trust me, I know how hard it can be to share such a personal experience with someone else. But in reading this book I hope you've found solace and peace knowing that you aren't alone.

As crazy, funny, emotional, traumatic, or educational the sexident, we must allow the same grace for our healing process.

Some of us prefer to share our sexidents with someone close, while others prefer to keep their experiences more private. Whatever your preference, sharing your experience in any way can help you feel less isolated.

In addition to what you took away from each story, here are some tools and resources you can use, wherever you are on your journey, to support healing from your sexident. Many of these truly helped me.

Speak to someone you trust:

A safe and confidential environment where you can share any of your thoughts and emotions related to the sexident is sometimes all you need.

Talking about your experiences with someone you trust can be immensely healing and validating. It provides an opportunity to express your thoughts, emotions, and fears, and to receive support and empathy from another person who cares about your well-being.

When considering who to confide in, think about people in your life who have demonstrated understanding, empathy, and unconditional support. It could be a family member such as your mom or sister(I thank God for mine,) a close friend, a mentor, or even a support group or organization that focuses on sexual trauma. It's with great hope that at the release of this book, a support group dedicated specifically to sexident survivors will be born.

The important thing is to choose someone you feel 100% comfortable sharing with. This person should be non-judgmental, compassionate, and willing to listen without interrupting or invalidating your feelings. By opening up to someone you trust, you create an opportunity to release the weight of your experiences and find solace in knowing that you are not alone.

Sharing your story with a trusted person can also lead to unexpected connections and discoveries. They may have had a similar experience, or they may know someone who has. Knowing that you're not alone and that others have navigated similar challenges and successfully healed can be immensely comforting and empowering.

It's worth noting that not everyone may be equipped to provide the level of support and understanding you need. Some individuals, even well-intentioned ones, might struggle to comprehend the depth of your experience or respond in a way that meets your needs. If this occurs, it is essential to reach out to other trusted individuals or seek professional help, as they can offer you the guidance and support you require.

Remember, you have options when it comes to finding support. Reach out to the individuals or organizations that resonate with you, and trust your intuition in choosing who to confide in. Healing and finding solace can be facilitated through connection and open communication with those who genuinely care about your well-being. Trust that there are people out there who will listen, understand, and support you unconditionally on your journey to healing and resilience.

Therapy:

Sometimes, you need some professional help to overcome a sexident, especially if it was traumatic for you. This is totally okay. Therapy can help you to make sense of your sexident. This reduces the emotional impact of the memories so the intrusive, or negative thoughts, flashbacks, and nightmares eventually go away. It may take some time, but you got this.

Navigating the aftermath of a sexident can be incredibly challenging. The trauma associated with such an experience can have a lasting impact on your mental and emotional well-being. While it's natural to try and cope on your own, seeking professional help through therapy is a wise and courageous choice.

Therapy provides a safe and supportive environment where you can openly express your thoughts, feelings, and fears related to the sexident. A skilled therapist, experienced in trauma work, can guide you through the healing process, helping you understand and make sense of your memories. They can provide you with tools to cope with emotional distress and learn healthy ways of managing the intrusive thoughts, flashbacks, and nightmares that may be affecting your daily life.

One therapeutic approach commonly used in trauma-focused therapy is cognitive behavioral therapy (CBT). This approach emphasizes identifying and modifying negative thought patterns and deeply ingrained beliefs that may be contributing to the emotional impact of the sexident. Through CBT, you can develop new ways of thinking and responding to your experiences, fostering a sense of empowerment and resilience.

While therapy can't erase the past or make the memories disappear entirely, it offers a path to healing, transformation, and resilience. It's important to remember that healing takes time and each person's journey is unique. Be patient and compassionate with yourself throughout the process.

Betterhelp.com and Talkspace.com are great platforms to seek professional help just right for you.

Journaling

Journaling serves as a powerful and therapeutic tool for nurturing a deep connection with oneself and exploring one's emotions. When it comes to acknowledging and addressing one's sexident, it is essential not to suppress or ignore the thoughts and emotions associated with it. This challenging experience calls for a constructive response, rather than pushing it down or denying its existence.

Instead, view journaling as a metaphorical window into your own mind. By putting pen to paper and expressing your emotions and thoughts, you can begin to understand and unravel the layers of your experience. Allow your words to flow freely, without judgment or restrictions. This writing process can bring clarity and deeper insight, offering you the opportunity to make sense of your emotions and experiences.

Once you have poured your thoughts onto the pages of your journal, take the time to read them back to yourself. This act of reflection allows you to witness your personal journey from a new perspective and acknowledge the progress you have made in understanding and processing your feelings. Allow yourself permission to honor the growth and self-discovery that you achieved through the act of journaling.

In doing so, you may come across lessons or key insights gained from your experience. Look for patterns, themes, or transformative moments that emerge from your reflection. Discovering these valuable lessons can contribute to your personal growth and empower you to navigate similar

Journaling

challenges in the future with wisdom and resilience.

So, grab your journal, pour your heart onto its pages, and let it become a trusted companion on your journey of self-discovery and healing. Embrace the transformative power of journaling as you uncover the lessons hidden within your own story.

In addition to journaling my thoughts, The Come As You Are Workbook: A Practical Guide To The Science of Sex by Emily Nagoski and Sex: An Erotic Journal for Sexual Inspiration and Exploration by Margaret Hurst and Jordan LaRousse are two journals that helped me immensely during my healing journey.

Resources

Communicate with your partner:

Experiencing a sexident with your partner can pose additional challenges, as it involves navigating the impact on your relationship and finding ways to support each other through the healing process. Communication becomes crucial during this time, and being mindful of each other's needs and emotions can contribute to a healthier and more compassionate connection.

One fundamental aspect of supporting each other after a sexident is open and honest communication. Be transparent with your partner about what you're feeling, what you need, and what feels comfortable for you as you heal. Both of you must have a clear understanding of each other's boundaries, triggers, and limitations. Sharing this information can help foster a sense of safety and trust within the relationship.

As you communicate with your partner, make sure to ask for patience and reassurance. Healing from a sexident can be a complex journey, and it's normal to experience ups and downs along the way. Let your partner know that you may have moments of vulnerability and that their understanding and support are vital in navigating those challenges. Being patient with yourself and each other can create a space for growth and healing within the relationship.

Remember that your partner may also have their own emotions and reactions to navigate in response to the sexident. Encourage open dialogue and active listening, which can foster understanding and empathy on both sides.

Communicate with your partner

Honesty and vulnerability can strengthen your bond and create a resilient foundation for moving forward together.

Erotic workshops like "The Sexy Journal for Partners" with Bria Price (private sessions and group classes offered at Briacprice.com) can provide valuable insights and guidance for couples navigating the aftermath of a sexident.

Remember, healing is a process that takes time, and it's not a linear journey. By prioritizing open communication, patience, and understanding within your relationship, you can create a supportive environment where both you and your partner can heal and grow together.

Resources

Reconnect to your body:

Reconnecting with your body after a sexident is an essential part of the healing process. Your body may have experienced a profound disconnect, and it may take time to regain a sense of comfort and familiarity with your physical self. Remember that the journey to reconnecting with your body is unique to you, and there is no right or wrong way to approach it. What matters is finding what feels right for you and honoring your personal boundaries and needs.

Practicing celibacy until you feel safe and ready to engage sexually again can be an empowering choice. Taking time to prioritize your emotional and physical well-being allows you to establish a solid foundation of safety and self-trust. It gives you the freedom to explore your desires, boundaries, and comfort levels without external pressures.

Starting slowly as you reconnect with your body can help you regain a sense of agency and ownership over your own experiences. Begin by simply feeling the sensations in your body without judgment or expectation. This mindful approach allows you to return to yourself and find a more grounded sense of presence. Whether it's through yoga, meditation, masturbation, or dance, find a practice that resonates with you and allows you to explore the connection between your body and mind.

Yoga can be a powerful tool for reconnecting with your body. It invites you to pay attention to the sensations, movements, and breath within your body. By practicing yoga, you can cultivate a deeper awareness of your physicality, release tension and trauma stored in your muscles, and reconnect with your body gently and compassionately. Visit your local studio, or tune in at home, on Youtube with the amazing @AriannaElizabeth. Meditation, on the other hand, allows you to quiet your mind and focus on the present moment. This practice can help you become more attuned to the sensations in your body, as well as cultivate a sense of calm and self-acceptance. By regularly practicing meditation, you can develop a deeper connection with yourself and your physical being. I've been living by the Bettersleep app for the past 7+ years. They offer guided meditation, hypnosis, and more. The Calm app is a great meditation tool as well.

Masturbation can also be a valuable tool for rediscovering pleasure and intimacy with your body. It allows you to explore what feels good to you, and it can help you rebuild a positive relationship with your sexuality. Remember that self-pleasure is a personal and individual experience, and there is no right or wrong way to engage with it. Allow yourself to take the time you need, be patient with yourself, and approach self-pleasure with curiosity and self-compassion. Amazon has a wide variety of sex toys to choose from for the ultimate pleasure.

Dance is another powerful avenue for reconnecting with your body. Movement can be a form of self-expression and a way to release emotions, tension, and trauma stored in your body. Whether you join a local pole dancing class or simply move to your favorite music in the privacy of your own space, allowing yourself to move freely and without judgment can help you reclaim your body as a source of joy and expression.

Remember, this journey of reconnecting with your body is deeply personal, and it may involve exploring various practices and activities until you find what resonates with you. Be gentle and patient with yourself as you navigate this process. Embrace self-care, self-compassion, and self-acceptance throughout your healing journey. Your body is a vessel of resilience that can heal and rediscover pleasure at any time. Trust in your body's innate wisdom and allow it to guide you towards a deeper reconnection with yourself.

Laugh about it!

While healing from a sexident can be a challenging and emotionally charged process, it's important to remember that laughter can also hold a place in our healing journey. Often, some of our most difficult experiences can be transformed into humorous anecdotes that we can reflect on and find amusement in. By finding a way to laugh about our sexidents, we can create a sense of lightness in the face of adversity.

It's important to note that laughing about a sexident doesn't mean dismissing or trivializing the significance of what happened. Some sexidents may have been genuinely unpleasant or traumatic experiences. However, finding humor in the aftermath doesn't diminish the seriousness of the event. Instead, it allows us to reframe our perspective and find a silver lining amidst our experiences.

Finding the humor or positive moments in an sexident can be a powerful way to reclaim our sense of self. It's about recognizing that even though the situation may have been difficult, we harbor the capacity to grow, learn, and become wiser as a result. By training ourselves to seek the positive that emerges out of negative events, we cultivate resilience and develop a mindset that can positively impact our minds and bodies.

When we find humor in our sexident experiences, it can bring us closer to our partners too. Laughing together can create a sense of solidarity and shared understanding. It allows us to release tension, lighten the emotional load, and cultivate a deeper connection. Sharing a laugh can be a

Laugh about it!

way to acknowledge the vulnerability and humanity in all of us, fostering a sense of acceptance and compassion in the relationship.
Of course, it's important to approach humor in a sexident context with sensitivity and respect for one another's boundaries. What one person may find funny, another may not. It's crucial to have open and honest communication with our partners to ensure that we're both comfortable and on the same page when it comes to finding humor in our shared experiences.

Let's be honest, some of our sexidents are downright hysterical. Again, it doesn't always mean that what happened was good; it may have been truly awful. Still, those experiences have made you stronger, and all the wiser.

UNTIL THE NEXT SEXIDENT...

Acknowledgment

Thank you to these beautiful souls who courageously shared their stories with me for this book. Especially during the heart of the pandemic when we weren't able to connect in person.

Writing this book made healing all the more worth it. I love each and every one of you.

About the Author:

Bria Price is a passionate author, teaching artist, and advocate for sexual confidence and wellness from Baltimore, MD. With two visually captivating poetry books, "Love is…" and "Sex is…," under her belt, her words flow effortlessly, resonating with readers, and inviting them to reflect on love, identity, and the complexities of sexuality.

Her impact extends beyond the written word. As a teaching artist, she facilitates dynamic workshops, including the popular "Sexy Journal" workshop, where participants can explore their desires and embrace their sexuality in a private or group session. You can reach out to Bria for more information or book a session at her website Briacprice.com.

www.ingramcontent.com/pod-product-compliance
Lightning Source LLC
Chambersburg PA
CBHW062043290426
44109CB00026B/2712